YOSEMITE TRVEL

GUIDE 2023

Discover The Natural Wonders And Outdoor Adventures Of Yosemite National Park

LINDA J. MOORE

Table Of Contents

Welcome To Yosemite

My last visit to Yosemite National Park was an experience that will stay with me for the rest of my life. The stunning scenery and natural beauty of the park left me in awe, and I felt a deep connection to the natural world that I had never experienced before.

As I drove towards the park, I was struck by the sheer size of the mountains that loomed ahead of me. The peaks were covered in snow, and the sunlight bouncing off the snow made the mountains appear almost ethereal. I could hardly believe that I was about to spend the next few days exploring this incredible wilderness.

When I arrived at the park entrance, I was greeted by a friendly ranger who gave me a map of the park and some advice on where to go. I decided to start my adventure by driving to Glacier Point, which offers some of the most breathtaking views in the park.

As I drove up the winding road towards Glacier Point, I was treated to stunning vistas of the Yosemite Valley below me. The valley was filled with towering trees, sparkling streams, and sheer granite cliffs that rose up towards the sky. I was amazed by the sheer size of everything around me and felt small in comparison to the grandeur of nature.

When I reached Glacier Point, I stepped out of my car and was immediately hit by the fresh mountain air. I could feel the cool breeze on my skin, and I took a deep breath, filling my lungs with the scent of pine trees and wildflowers. As I looked out at the view before me, I was completely speechless. The valley stretched out before me, and I could see all the way to Half Dome and Yosemite Falls in the distance. I felt as if I could see for miles and miles, and I was struck by the majesty of the natural world.

After spending some time taking in the view from Glacier Point, I decided to hike down into the valley itself. The trail was steep and rocky, but the scenery was so stunning that I hardly noticed the exertion. The trail wound through dense forests and across sparkling streams, and every turn offered a new and breathtaking view.

As I descended deeper into the valley, I began to feel a sense of calm and peace that I had never experienced before. The sounds of rushing water and rustling leaves were soothing, and the fresh scent of the forest filled my senses. I felt completely at one with nature, and I realized how important it is to protect and preserve the natural world.

When I finally reached the valley floor, I was greeted by an abundance of wildlife. Deer grazed in the meadows, and birds flitted through the trees. I even spotted a coyote slinking through the underbrush. I felt so grateful to be able to witness these creatures in their natural habitat, and it made me realize how much we stand to lose if we don't take care of the environment.

Over the next few days, I explored the park in depth, hiking to beautiful waterfalls, marveling at the enormous trees, and soaking in the natural hot springs. Every experience left me feeling more connected to the natural world, and I found myself wanting to do everything I could to protect it.

As my visit drew to a close, I felt a sense of sadness at having to leave this incredible wilderness behind. However, I also felt inspired to continue exploring the natural world and doing everything in my power to protect it. Yosemite had left an indelible mark on my heart and soul, and I knew that I would never forget this incredible experience.

CHAPTER 1

INTRODUCTION

Brief History

Yosemite National Park is a world-famous destination located in the western region of the United States. Spanning more than 1,200 square miles in California's Sierra Nevada Mountains, Yosemite is known for its breathtaking natural beauty, including towering granite cliffs, ancient sequoia trees, and sparkling waterfalls. However, the history of Yosemite goes back much further than its creation as a national park in 1890.

The first inhabitants of the Yosemite Valley were the Ahwahneechee people, who lived in the area for thousands of years. The Ahwahneechee were a branch of the larger Miwok tribe, and they relied on the natural resources of the valley for survival. They hunted deer, elk, and other game animals, and they gathered acorns, berries, and other plants from the surrounding forests.

In the early 1800s, European settlers began to explore the area, and they quickly realized the beauty and natural resources of the Yosemite Valley. However, it wasn't until the mid-1800s that Yosemite gained widespread attention as a tourist destination.

In 1855, a group of explorers led by a man named Lafayette Bunnell entered the valley and were struck by its beauty. Bunnell named the valley "Yosemite," which means "killer" in the language of the nearby Miwok tribe. The name referred to the fierce battles that took place between the Ahwahneechee and neighboring tribes.

Word of the valley's beauty spread, and soon tourists began to flock to the area. In 1864, President Abraham Lincoln signed the Yosemite Grant, which protected the valley and the Mariposa Grove of giant sequoia trees from development and ensured that they would remain public land for future generations to enjoy.

However, despite the protection afforded by the Yosemite Grant, the area continued to face threats from logging, mining, and other forms of development. In the early 1900s, conservationists led by naturalist John Muir fought to protect Yosemite from these threats, and their efforts were successful in securing greater protections for the area.

In 1916, President Woodrow Wilson signed the National Park Service Organic Act, which created the National Park Service and established it as a federal agency responsible for managing national parks and other protected areas. Yosemite was one of the first national parks to be established, and it remains one of the most popular and beloved parks in the country.

Over the years, Yosemite has faced many challenges, including wildfires, floods, and overcrowding. However, thanks to the efforts of dedicated conservationists and park rangers, the area has remained largely intact and continues to inspire visitors from around the world.

Today, Yosemite is home to a wide range of wildlife, including black bears, mountain lions, and coyotes. It is also home to some of the world's most famous rock climbing routes, including El Capitan and Half Dome. Visitors can hike, bike, fish, and camp in the park, and they can also enjoy ranger-led programs and educational exhibits that explore the history and natural wonders of the area.

While the history of Yosemite is complex and multifaceted, one thing is clear: this incredible natural wonder is a testament to the power of conservation and the importance of protecting our planet's natural resources. Yosemite is a reminder of the beauty and wonder of the natural world, and it continues to inspire awe and admiration in visitors from around the world.

Yosemite Weather

Yosemite National Park is situated in California's Sierra Nevada mountain range, and as such, it experiences a range of weather conditions throughout the year. From hot and dry summers to cold and snowy winters, the weather in Yosemite can have a significant impact on visitors' experiences and activities.

Summer is the busiest time of year in Yosemite, with warm temperatures and clear skies making it the perfect time to explore the park's hiking trails and scenic vistas. Average temperatures during the summer months range from the high 70s to low 90s Fahrenheit, with occasional heatwaves bringing temperatures above 100 degrees Fahrenheit. However, despite the warm temperatures, afternoon thunderstorms are not uncommon in the summer, particularly in the high country areas of the park.

Fall is a popular time to visit Yosemite, as the summer crowds have dissipated, and the changing colors of the leaves make for stunning scenery. Average temperatures during the fall months range from the mid-40s to mid-70s Fahrenheit, and precipitation is relatively low. However, visitors should be aware that the weather can be unpredictable, and snowstorms are not unheard of in October and November.

Winter in Yosemite can be harsh, with snow and cold temperatures making many of the park's roads and trails impassable. The park's high country areas, including

Tuolumne Meadows, are closed to vehicles during the winter months, and visitors must access them on skis or snowshoes. Average temperatures during the winter months range from the low 30s to mid-40s Fahrenheit, and snowfall can range from a few inches to several feet. However, even in the midst of winter, visitors can still enjoy the park's lower elevations, including Yosemite Valley, which typically receives less snow than the higher elevations.

Spring is a beautiful time to visit Yosemite, with wildflowers blooming and waterfalls at their peak flow. However, visitors should be aware that the weather can be unpredictable, with warm, sunny days giving way to cold, rainy ones. Average temperatures during the spring months range from the mid-30s to mid-60s Fahrenheit, and precipitation is relatively high.

One of the most significant weather-related concerns in Yosemite is wildfires. The park is prone to wildfires, particularly during the dry summer months. In recent years, wildfires have caused significant damage to the park, with smoke and poor air quality impacting visitors' experiences.

Visitors should be aware of the risk of wildfires and should check the park's website for up-to-date information on fire restrictions and closures.

In addition to weather-related concerns, visitors to Yosemite should also be aware of altitude-related issues. Many of the park's popular attractions, including Half Dome and Glacier Point, are at high elevations, which can cause altitude sickness in some visitors. Symptoms of altitude sickness can include headaches, nausea, and shortness of breath. Visitors should take precautions to prevent altitude sickness, including staying hydrated, avoiding alcohol, and allowing time for acclimatization.

Best Time to Visit

Summer is the busiest time of year in Yosemite, with warm temperatures and clear skies making it the perfect time to explore the park's hiking trails and scenic vistas. Many of the park's attractions, including Tioga Road, Glacier Point, and Mariposa Grove, are accessible during the summer months. However, visitors should be aware that summer is also the peak season for crowds, and popular areas like

Yosemite Valley can be crowded with tourists. Visitors should plan ahead and make reservations for accommodations, camping, and activities well in advance.

Fall is a popular time to visit Yosemite, as the summer crowds have dissipated, and the changing colors of the leaves make for stunning scenery. The park's fall colors typically peak in late October or early November, making it a perfect time for photography and hiking. Visitors can also take advantage of the park's quieter atmosphere and enjoy peaceful moments at popular attractions. However, visitors should be aware that the weather can be unpredictable, and snowstorms are not unheard of in October and November.

Winter in Yosemite can be a magical time, with snow and cold temperatures turning the park into a winter wonderland. The park's high country areas, including Tuolumne Meadows, are closed to vehicles during the winter months, but visitors can still enjoy winter activities such as cross-country skiing, snowshoeing, and ice-skating in Yosemite Valley. The park's waterfalls, including Yosemite Falls and Bridalveil Fall, are also spectacular in winter when they freeze over. However, visitors should be prepared for winter conditions, including road closures, chain requirements, and limited services. It is important to check weather and road conditions before visiting in winter.

Spring is a beautiful time to visit Yosemite, with wildflowers blooming and waterfalls at their peak flow. The park's waterfalls typically reach their peak flow in late May or early June, making it a popular time for waterfall hikes and photography. Visitors can also enjoy milder temperatures and fewer crowds before the summer rush. However, visitors should be aware that the weather can be unpredictable, with warm, sunny days giving way to cold, rainy ones.

In addition to seasonal considerations, visitors should also be aware of special events and activities in the park that may influence the best time to visit. For example, the annual Yosemite Facelift event, which encourages volunteers to clean up litter and debris in the park, takes place in late September, making it a great time to visit and participate in community service. The Yosemite Valley

Music Festival, held in July, features performances by musicians from around the world and is a popular event for music lovers.

How To Get There

- **By Car:**

Driving is one of the most popular ways to get to Yosemite, as it offers the most flexibility and allows visitors to explore the park at their own pace. From San Francisco, take Interstate 580 East to Interstate 205 East, which will merge with Interstate 5 North. Take Exit 461 to Highway 120 East, which will take you into the park via the Big Oak Flat entrance. From Los Angeles, take Interstate 5 North to Highway 99 North, then take Highway 140 East into the park via the Arch Rock entrance.

- **By Bus:**

Several bus companies offer transportation to Yosemite from major cities in California, including San Francisco and Los Angeles. YARTS (Yosemite Area Regional Transportation System) provides service from Merced, Fresno, and other nearby communities to the park's visitor centers. Greyhound also offers service to Merced, from which visitors can take YARTS to Yosemite.

● **By Train:**

While there is no direct train service to Yosemite, Amtrak offers service to several nearby cities, including Merced and Fresno. From these cities, visitors can take YARTS or rent a car to reach the park.

● **By Air:**

The closest major airports to Yosemite are San Francisco International Airport and Fresno Yosemite International Airport. Both airports offer car rentals, and visitors can drive or take public transportation to the park. Additionally, the Mammoth Yosemite Airport, located about an hour and a half south of the park, offers limited service from several cities in California.

Once you have arrived at Yosemite, there are several transportation options available to explore the park. Private vehicles are allowed in the park, but visitors should be aware that parking can be limited, especially during peak season. The park offers free shuttle service throughout Yosemite Valley and Tuolumne Meadows, which is a convenient and environmentally-friendly way to explore the park without worrying about parking.

15 Reasons To Plan a Trip To Yosemite As Your Next Vacation Destination

1. **Stunning Scenery:** Yosemite is known for its breathtaking natural beauty, including towering granite cliffs, cascading waterfalls, and pristine wilderness areas.

2. **World-Famous Landmarks:** The park is home to several iconic landmarks, including Half Dome, El Capitan, and Yosemite Falls, that are recognized around the world.

3. **Diverse Wildlife:** Visitors to Yosemite can encounter a wide variety of wildlife, including black bears, mountain lions, deer, coyotes, and more.

4. **Hiking Opportunities:** Yosemite boasts over 750 miles of trails, ranging from easy strolls to challenging hikes, that offer stunning views of the park's natural beauty.

5. **Rock Climbing:** Yosemite is considered one of the world's premier destinations for rock climbing, with thousands of routes for climbers of all skill levels.

6. **Water Activities:** The park's many lakes and rivers offer opportunities for fishing, kayaking, rafting, and swimming.

7. **Skiing and Snowboarding:** During the winter months, visitors can enjoy skiing and snowboarding at Yosemite's Badger Pass Ski Area.

8. **Historic Sites:** Yosemite is home to several historic sites, including the Ahwahnee Hotel and the Yosemite Valley Chapel, that offer a glimpse into the park's past.

9. **Art and Photography:** Yosemite has inspired generations of artists and photographers, and visitors can enjoy exhibits and workshops showcasing the park's natural beauty.

10. **Stargazing:** Yosemite's dark skies make it a prime location for stargazing, with several designated viewing areas throughout the park.

11. **Camping:** With over 1,500 campsites and 13 campgrounds, Yosemite offers a wide range of camping options, from backcountry wilderness camping to full-service RV sites.

12. **Lodging:** Visitors can choose from a variety of lodging options, including historic hotels, rustic cabins, and modern lodges.

13. **Family-Friendly Activities:** Yosemite offers a range of family-friendly activities, including Junior Ranger programs, guided hikes, and educational exhibits.

14. **Accessibility:** The park has made significant efforts to make its facilities and trails more accessible to visitors with disabilities, including wheelchair-accessible hiking trails and shuttle buses.

15. **Unforgettable Experience:** Above all, a trip to Yosemite offers an unforgettable experience, with the chance to disconnect from the stresses of daily life and connect with nature in a truly unique and awe-inspiring setting.

CHAPTER 2

TIPS AND CONSIDERATIONS

Visiting Yosemite on a Budget

- **Plan your trip in advance**

The first step to visiting Yosemite on a budget is to plan your trip well in advance. Yosemite is a popular destination, especially during peak season, which runs from May through September. During this time, the park can get crowded, and prices for lodging and activities can skyrocket. To avoid this, plan your trip for the shoulder season, which runs from April to May and September to October. During this time, the weather is still pleasant, and the crowds are smaller.

- **Choose budget-friendly accommodations**

One of the most significant expenses when visiting Yosemite is lodging. The park offers a range of accommodations, from campsites to luxury hotels, but these can be costly. To save money, consider staying outside the park and driving in for day trips. There are plenty of affordable lodging options in nearby towns like

Mariposa, Oakhurst, and Groveland. These towns offer budget-friendly hotels, motels, and vacation rentals, many of which are just a short drive from the park entrance.

- **Take advantage of free activities**

Yosemite offers a range of free activities that allow you to experience the park's natural beauty without spending a dime. Some of the best free activities include hiking, picnicking, and wildlife viewing. There are over 800 miles of trails in Yosemite, ranging from easy walks to strenuous hikes. The park also has several picnic areas where you can enjoy a meal with a view, and you're likely to see a range of wildlife, from deer to black bears.

- **Buy a National Parks Pass**

If you're planning on visiting multiple national parks during your trip, consider buying a National Parks Pass. This pass gives you access to all national parks and federal recreational lands for one year and can save you a significant amount of money. A single-day pass to Yosemite costs $35 per vehicle, while an annual pass costs $80 and gives you access to over 2,000 federal recreation sites across the country.

- **Bring your own food and drinks**

One of the easiest ways to save money when visiting Yosemite is to bring your own food and drinks. The park has several grocery stores and restaurants, but these can be expensive, especially if you're on a tight budget. Instead, pack a cooler with snacks, sandwiches, and drinks, and bring a portable stove or grill to cook meals at your campsite or picnic area.

- **Rent camping gear**

Camping is a great way to experience Yosemite's natural beauty while staying on a budget. However, if you don't have your own camping gear, renting can be costly. To save money, consider renting camping gear from a local outfitter. Many outfitters offer affordable rentals, including tents, sleeping bags, and backpacks, and some even offer packages that include everything you need for a camping trip.

- **Take advantage of free shuttle buses**

Yosemite offers a free shuttle bus service that makes it easy to explore the park without a car. The shuttle buses run on several routes, including the Yosemite Valley Shuttle, which stops at all major points of interest in the valley.

Taking the shuttle bus can save you money on gas and parking fees, and it's an excellent way to reduce your carbon footprint.

- **Avoid peak season**

As mentioned earlier, visiting Yosemite during peak season can be expensive. In addition to higher lodging and activity prices, you may also have to deal with crowded trails, long wait times, and limited availability. To save money and avoid the crowds, consider visiting Yosemite during the off-season. Not only will you have a better chance of finding affordable lodging and activities, but you'll also have a more peaceful and relaxing experience.

- **Use your own transportation**

If you have your own vehicle, using it to explore Yosemite can be a cost-effective option. While there are shuttle buses available, having your own car gives you the flexibility to explore the park at your own pace and on your own schedule. Additionally, you won't have to worry about paying for shuttle tickets or waiting for the next available bus. However, it's important to note that parking can be limited in some areas, so be prepared to arrive early or park farther away and walk or take a shuttle to your destination.

● **Take advantage of ranger-led programs**

Yosemite offers a variety of ranger-led programs that are free or low-cost. These programs provide an opportunity to learn about the park's natural and cultural history, as well as participate in guided hikes and other activities. Some popular programs include stargazing, bird watching, and nature walks. Check the park's website or visitor center for a schedule of upcoming programs and events.

Getting Around Yosemite

I. Shuttle Buses

Yosemite National Park offers a free shuttle bus service that is a convenient and affordable way to get around the park. The shuttle buses run on several routes, including the Yosemite Valley Shuttle, which stops at all major points of interest in the valley, and the Glacier Point Shuttle, which takes visitors to the Glacier Point overlook.

Using the shuttle buses is free of charge and can save you money on gas and parking fees. Additionally, it's an excellent way to reduce your carbon footprint and help preserve Yosemite's natural environment.

II. Private Vehicle

If you prefer to drive yourself, having your own vehicle gives you the flexibility to explore Yosemite at your own pace and on your own schedule. However, there are some things to keep in mind to avoid unnecessary expenses.

First, make sure to plan your route ahead of time to avoid backtracking or getting lost. Yosemite's winding mountain roads can be confusing, and some areas have limited parking availability, especially during peak season. Check the park's website for updated road conditions and closures. Second, be aware of parking fees. Parking in Yosemite can be expensive, and some areas have limited parking availability. If you plan to park in Yosemite Valley, consider arriving early to secure a spot or park farther away and take the shuttle bus.

III. Biking

Biking is a fun and eco-friendly way to explore Yosemite National Park. The park has over 12 miles of paved bike paths, including the Yosemite Valley Bike Path, which follows the Merced River and offers stunning views of Yosemite's granite cliffs and waterfalls.

You can bring your own bike or rent one from several rental shops in Yosemite Valley, including Yosemite Valley Bikes and Sport. Bike rentals start at around $12 per hour or $30 per day. Additionally, you can bring your bike on the shuttle buses, which have bike racks.

IV. Hiking

Yosemite is famous for its hiking trails, which range from easy strolls to strenuous hikes. Hiking is a free and rewarding way to explore Yosemite's natural beauty and get some exercise at the same time.

However, it's important to be prepared and have the right gear. Wear comfortable, sturdy shoes and bring plenty of water, snacks, and sun protection. Additionally, make sure to check the weather forecast and trail conditions before heading out, and always follow park regulations and safety guidelines.

V. Tours and Guided Activities

Yosemite offers a variety of tours and guided activities that can help you make the most of your visit. From guided hikes to photography workshops, there's something for everyone. However, these activities can be expensive, so it's important to choose wisely and plan ahead.

Some popular tours and activities include the Valley Floor Tour, which takes visitors on a two-hour tour of Yosemite Valley, and the Ansel Adams Gallery Photography Walks, which offer guided photography sessions in the park. Prices for these activities vary, with some tours costing up to $50 per person.

VI. Rafting

Rafting is a popular activity in Yosemite, and there are several companies that offer guided tours down the Merced River. This is a great way to experience Yosemite's natural beauty from a different perspective and get some adrenaline pumping at the same time.

However, rafting tours can be expensive, with prices starting at around $50 per person for a two-hour tour. Additionally, make sure to choose a reputable company and check the company's safety record and equipment before booking your tour.

VII.Hitchhiking

While not a recommended method of transportation, hitchhiking is an option for those on a tight budget. However, it's important to note that hitchhiking is not allowed within Yosemite National Park, and hitchhikers are subject to fines and penalties.

If you do choose to hitchhike outside of the park, make sure to use caution and common sense. Only accept rides from people you trust and feel comfortable with, and always let someone know where you're going and when you expect to return.

VIII. Ride Sharing

Ride sharing services such as Uber and Lyft are not available within Yosemite National Park. However, there are some private transportation companies that offer rides to and from the park, as well as tours and other services.

One such company is Yosemite Area Regional Transportation System (YARTS), which provides public transportation to and from Yosemite Valley and other areas around the park. Fares start at around $10 per person, depending on the distance traveled.

Another option is Yosemite Valley Shuttle, which offers private tours and transportation services within the park. Prices vary depending on the length of the tour and the number of people in your group.

IX. Camping

Camping is a popular way to explore Yosemite on a budget, and there are several campgrounds within the park that offer affordable accommodations. Prices for camping start at around $20 per night, depending on the campground and time of year.

Additionally, renting camping gear can save you money if you don't have your own equipment. Several rental shops in

Yosemite Valley offer tents, sleeping bags, and other camping gear for rent at reasonable prices.

X. Walking

Finally, one of the easiest and most affordable ways to get around Yosemite is by walking. Many of the park's attractions, such as Yosemite Falls and El Capitan, are easily accessible on foot from Yosemite Valley.

Walking is also a great way to experience Yosemite's natural beauty up close and at your own pace. However, be aware that some areas may be inaccessible or unsafe for pedestrians, so always follow park regulations and safety guidelines.

Shopping in Yosemite

- **Plan ahead**

Before your trip to Yosemite, research what items you might need and where to buy them. Bring essential items from home, such as sunscreen, insect repellent, and toiletries, to avoid overpaying for them in the park.

Additionally, consider bringing your own snacks and water bottles to save money on food and beverages. Many of the park's trails and attractions have water refill stations, so you can easily fill up your bottle for free.

- **Shop at the Yosemite Valley Store**

The Yosemite Valley Store is the largest store in the park and offers a wide range of products, from groceries to souvenirs to camping gear. Prices at the store are generally higher than outside the park, but it's still a good option for visitors who need to purchase necessities.

The store also offers a variety of deals and promotions throughout the year, such as discounts on camping gear during the off-season. Check the store's website or ask at the front desk for current promotions.

- **Visit the Ansel Adams Gallery**

The Ansel Adams Gallery, located in Yosemite Valley, features the works of renowned photographer Ansel Adams as well as other photographers and artists. While the gallery does offer expensive limited edition prints, it also has a selection of affordable prints, postcards, and other souvenirs.

Visitors can also attend free photography workshops and lectures offered by the gallery. These workshops provide a great opportunity to learn about photography and take stunning photos of the park.

● **Check out the Yosemite Art Center**

The Yosemite Art Center, also located in Yosemite Valley, offers art classes, workshops, and exhibits featuring local artists. Visitors can purchase affordable prints, pottery, jewelry, and other art items made by the center's artists.

The art center also offers free classes and events throughout the year, such as drawing and painting workshops and live music performances. Check the center's website or ask at the front desk for current events and schedules.

● **Shop at the Yosemite Village Store**

The Yosemite Village Store, located in the Yosemite Village, offers a selection of souvenirs, clothing, and gifts. Prices at the store are generally higher than outside the park, but it's a convenient option for visitors who want to purchase souvenirs.

The store also offers a variety of deals and promotions throughout the year, such as discounts on clothing and gifts during the off-season. Check the store's website or ask at the front desk for current promotions.

- **Visit the Pioneer Yosemite History Center**

The Pioneer Yosemite History Center, located in Wawona, offers a glimpse into the history of Yosemite and the surrounding area. Visitors can explore historic buildings and artifacts and learn about the early settlers and Native Americans who lived in the area.

The history center also has a gift shop that offers affordable souvenirs, such as postcards, books, and Native American crafts. Visitors can also attend free events and demonstrations, such as blacksmithing and basket weaving.

- **Shop at the Curry Village Store**

The Curry Village Store, located in Curry Village, offers a selection of souvenirs, clothing, and gifts. Prices at the store are generally higher than outside the park, but it's a convenient option for visitors who want to purchase souvenirs.

The store also offers a variety of deals and promotions throughout the year, such as discounts on clothing and gifts during the off-season. Check the store's website or ask at the front desk for current promotions.

● **Visit the Tuolumne Meadows Store**

The Tuolumne Meadows Store, located in the Tuolumne Meadows area of the park, offers a variety of products, including groceries, souvenirs, and camping gear. Prices at the store are generally higher than outside the park, but it's a convenient option for visitors who are staying in the Tuolumne Meadows area.

The store also offers a variety of deals and promotions throughout the year, such as discounts on camping gear during the off-season. Check the store's website or ask at the front desk for current promotions.

● **Shop at the Yosemite Conservancy Bookstore**

The Yosemite Conservancy Bookstore, located in Yosemite Valley, offers a selection of books, maps, and other educational materials about the park's history, geology, and ecology. Visitors can purchase affordable souvenirs, such as postcards and bookmarks, as well as more expensive items like art prints and jewelry.

All proceeds from the bookstore support the Yosemite Conservancy, a nonprofit organization that works to protect and preserve Yosemite National Park.

- **Shop outside the park**

If you're looking for a wider selection of products or lower prices, consider shopping outside the park. The nearest town to Yosemite is Mariposa, which has several grocery stores, drug stores, and other shops.

Another option is to stop at a Walmart or Target on your way to the park and purchase any necessary items before entering. Just be aware that the nearest Walmart is about an hour's drive from Yosemite, so plan accordingly.

5 Low-Cost Yosemite Hotel Options

1. Yosemite Bug Rustic Mountain Resort

Located just 25 miles from Yosemite National Park, the Yosemite Bug Rustic Mountain Resort offers a unique and affordable lodging experience. This rustic resort features a variety of accommodation options, including private cabins, dorm rooms, and even tents. Prices for private cabins start at around $150 per night, while dorm rooms start at just $38 per night.

Despite its low prices, the Yosemite Bug Rustic Mountain Resort offers a range of amenities and activities, including a spa, a sauna, and a hot tub. The resort also has a restaurant on site that serves a range of delicious meals, including vegetarian and vegan options.

2. Yosemite View Lodge

The Yosemite View Lodge is a popular choice for visitors looking for affordable accommodation near Yosemite National Park. Located just two miles from the park's west entrance, the lodge offers stunning views of the surrounding mountains and the Merced River. Rooms at the lodge start at around $150 per night.

Despite its low prices, the Yosemite View Lodge offers a range of amenities, including a heated outdoor pool, a hot tub, and a fitness center. The lodge also has a restaurant on site that serves breakfast, lunch, and dinner.

3. Cedar Lodge

Located just eight miles from Yosemite National Park's west entrance, Cedar Lodge offers comfortable accommodation at an affordable price. The lodge features a range of room types, including standard rooms, suites, and cabins. Prices for standard rooms start at around $130 per night.

Cedar Lodge offers a range of amenities, including a seasonal outdoor pool, a hot tub, and a restaurant. The lodge also offers free Wi-Fi throughout the property.

4. Yosemite Southgate Hotel and Suites

Located just 14 miles from Yosemite National Park's south entrance, the Yosemite Southgate Hotel and Suites offers comfortable accommodation at an affordable price. The hotel features a range of room types, including standard rooms, suites, and even apartments. Prices for standard rooms start at around $110 per night.

The Yosemite Southgate Hotel and Suites offers a range of amenities, including an outdoor pool, a hot tub, and a fitness center. The hotel also offers a complimentary breakfast each morning.

5. Indian Flat RV Park

For visitors looking for a unique and affordable lodging option, the Indian Flat RV Park offers a range of accommodation options, including cabins, RV sites, and tent sites. Located just 20 miles from Yosemite National Park's west entrance, the RV park offers stunning views of the surrounding mountains and the Merced River.

Prices for cabins at Indian Flat RV Park start at around $100 per night, while RV sites start at just $45 per night. The park also offers a range of amenities, including a seasonal outdoor pool, a hot tub, and a camp store.

5 Luxurious Places To Stay In Yosemite

1)   The Majestic Yosemite Hotel

Formerly known as the Ahwahnee Hotel, The Majestic Yosemite Hotel is one of the most iconic and luxurious lodging options in Yosemite National Park. Built in 1927, this stunning hotel is located in the heart of the park and offers breathtaking views of Yosemite Valley. Rooms at The Majestic Yosemite Hotel start at around $500 per night. Despite its historic charm, The Majestic Yosemite Hotel offers a range of modern amenities, including a fitness center, a spa, and a heated outdoor pool. The hotel also has several restaurants on site, including The Ahwahnee Dining Room, which offers fine dining in an elegant setting.

2) Tenaya Lodge at Yosemite

Located just outside the park's south entrance, Tenaya Lodge at Yosemite offers a luxurious stay in a stunning mountain setting. This upscale lodge features a range of room types, from standard rooms to suites and cabins. Prices for rooms at Tenaya Lodge start at around $300 per night.

Tenaya Lodge offers a range of amenities, including a spa, a fitness center, and several dining options. The lodge also has a heated outdoor pool and a hot tub, as well as an ice skating rink in the winter months.

3) Rush Creek Lodge at Yosemite

Rush Creek Lodge at Yosemite is a luxury resort located just outside the park's west entrance. This beautiful lodge features a range of room types, including suites and family rooms, all of which offer stunning views of the surrounding mountains. Prices for rooms at Rush Creek Lodge start at around $350 per night.

The resort offers a range of amenities, including a spa, a fitness center, and a heated outdoor pool. The lodge also has several dining options, including the popular Rush Creek Restaurant, which serves farm-to-table cuisine.

4) Château du Sureau

Located just outside the park's south entrance, Château du Sureau is a luxurious boutique hotel that offers an intimate and elegant stay. This stunning hotel features just 10 rooms, each of which is uniquely decorated with antique furnishings and luxurious fabrics. Prices for rooms at Château du Sureau start at around $600 per night.

The hotel offers a range of amenities, including a spa, a fitness center, and a heated outdoor pool. The on-site restaurant, Erna's Elderberry House, is one of the best fine dining restaurants in the region, serving French and European cuisine made with locally sourced ingredients.

5) Evergreen Lodge at Yosemite

Located just outside the park's west entrance, Evergreen Lodge at Yosemite offers a luxurious stay in a rustic and charming setting. This beautiful lodge features a range of room types, including cabins and suites, all of which are beautifully decorated with rustic furnishings and modern amenities. Prices for rooms at Evergreen Lodge start at around $400 per night.

The lodge offers a range of amenities, including a spa, a fitness center, and a heated outdoor pool. The lodge also has a restaurant on site, the Camp Restaurant, which serves farm-to-table cuisine made with locally sourced ingredients.

CHAPTER 3

TOP 5 EVENTS IN YOSEMITE TO ATTEND

1. Yosemite Valley Floor Tour

One of the best ways to experience Yosemite is to take a guided tour of the valley floor. The valley floor tour is a 2-hour tour that takes visitors through the heart of the valley, showcasing some of the park's most iconic landmarks, including Half Dome, El Capitan, and Yosemite Falls. The tour is led by a park ranger who will provide insight into the history and geology of the park. The best time to take the valley floor tour is during the spring or fall when the weather is mild, and the crowds are smaller.

2. Yosemite Firefall

The Yosemite Firefall is a natural phenomenon that occurs during the winter months when the setting sun illuminates Horsetail Fall, creating a glowing "firefall" effect. This event only occurs for a few weeks each year, typically in February, and is a must-see for anyone visiting Yosemite during this time. The best time to view the Firefall is in the late afternoon, just before sunset, when the sun's rays are angled just right to light up the waterfall.

3. Yosemite Moonbow

Another unique natural phenomenon that occurs in Yosemite is the Moonbow. A Moonbow is a rainbow that is created by the light of the moon rather than the sun. Yosemite's Moonbow can be seen at the base of Yosemite Falls during the spring months when the water flow is high, and the moon is full. The best time to view the Moonbow is after dark, so bring a flashlight or headlamp to light your way.

4. Yosemite Stargazing

Yosemite is home to some of the darkest skies in the country, making it an excellent location for stargazing. Visitors can participate in ranger-led stargazing programs or take a guided tour of the park's nighttime skies. The best time to view the stars in Yosemite is during the summer months when the weather is warm and clear. However, stargazing is possible year-round, so bring warm clothing and a blanket to stay comfortable.

5. Yosemite Photography Workshops

Yosemite's stunning natural beauty and unique geological formations make it a popular destination for photographers. The park offers a variety of photography workshops led by professional photographers who will provide instruction and guidance on how to capture the perfect shot. The best time to attend a photography workshop in Yosemite depends on what you want to photograph. Spring is an excellent time for capturing waterfalls and wildflowers, while fall is ideal for capturing the changing colors of the trees.

Top 5 Yosemite Experience

I. Hiking

Hiking is one of the best ways to experience Yosemite's natural beauty. The park offers hundreds of miles of hiking trails that range from easy walks to challenging treks. Some of the most popular hiking trails in Yosemite include the Mist Trail to Vernal and Nevada Falls, the Half Dome Trail, and the Four Mile Trail. Hiking in Yosemite allows you to get up close and personal with the park's natural wonders and is a great way to stay active while enjoying the great outdoors.

II. Waterfalls

Yosemite is home to some of the most spectacular waterfalls in the world. Some of the most famous waterfalls in the park include Yosemite Falls, Bridalveil Fall, and Vernal and Nevada Falls. Visitors can hike to the base of these waterfalls or view them from overlooks throughout the park. The best time to see the waterfalls is during the spring when the snowmelt is at its peak, and the waterfalls are flowing at their fullest.

III. Rock Climbing

Yosemite is world-renowned for its rock climbing, and it's a must-do activity for adventurous tourists. The park's granite cliffs, including El Capitan and Half Dome, attract climbers from all over the world. Whether you're a beginner or an experienced climber, there are routes for all skill levels. For those who are new to rock climbing, Yosemite offers guided climbing tours and lessons to get you started.

IV. Wildlife Watching

Yosemite is home to a variety of wildlife, including black bears, coyotes, bobcats, and mule deer. Visitors can spot these animals throughout the park, but the best place to see them is in the Yosemite Valley. The park offers ranger-led programs and guided tours to help visitors learn more about the park's wildlife and how to observe them safely.

V. Scenic Drives

If you're looking for a more relaxed way to experience Yosemite, take a scenic drive through the park. Yosemite offers some of the most beautiful drives in the country, including Tioga Road, which takes visitors through high alpine meadows and past pristine lakes, and Glacier Point Road, which offers stunning views of the Yosemite Valley and the park's iconic landmarks. Visitors can also take the Yosemite Valley Shuttle, which provides transportation to popular destinations throughout the valley.

3 Days Yosemite Itinerary

Day 1:

On your first day in Yosemite, start by exploring the Yosemite Valley. This is the most popular area of the park and home to some of its most iconic landmarks. Begin your day by driving to Tunnel View, where you can take in breathtaking views of El Capitan, Half Dome, and Yosemite Valley. From there, head to the Yosemite Valley Visitor Center to learn more about the park and pick up maps and information.

After visiting the visitor center, take a hike on the Mist Trail to Vernal and Nevada Falls. This 3.4-mile hike is strenuous but offers stunning views of two of Yosemite's most beautiful waterfalls. Be sure to bring plenty of water and snacks, as this hike can take several hours to complete.

After your hike, head back to the Yosemite Valley and enjoy a picnic lunch in one of the park's many picnic areas. In the afternoon, take a stroll along the Valley Loop Trail, which offers beautiful views of Yosemite Falls and other landmarks. Finish your day by watching the sunset from

Glacier Point, which offers panoramic views of the Yosemite Valley.

Expenses for Day 1:

- Entrance fee: $35 per vehicle (valid for seven days)
- Lunch: $10-15 per person (depending on your choice of food and drink)
- Snacks: $5-10 per person
- Parking fee at Glacier Point: $30 per vehicle

Day 2:

On your second day in Yosemite, head to the Tuolumne Meadows area of the park. This area is less crowded than the Yosemite Valley but offers breathtaking views of alpine meadows and the surrounding mountains.

Begin your day by driving on Tioga Road, which takes you through the heart of the Sierra Nevada mountains. Stop at Olmsted Point for stunning views of Tenaya Canyon and the surrounding granite peaks. From there, head to Tuolumne Meadows, where you can take a hike on the Cathedral Lakes Trail. This 8-mile roundtrip hike takes you through meadows, past streams, and offers breathtaking views of Cathedral Peak.

After your hike, head back to Tuolumne Meadows and enjoy a picnic lunch in one of the park's picnic areas. In the afternoon, explore the meadows on foot and take in the stunning scenery. Finish your day by driving back to the Yosemite Valley and watching the sunset from the El Capitan picnic area.

Expenses for Day 2:

- Gasoline: $20-30 (depending on your vehicle and gas prices)
- Lunch: $10-15 per person
- Snacks: $5-10 per person

Day 3:

On your third and final day in Yosemite, head to the Mariposa Grove of Giant Sequoias. This area of the park is home to over 500 mature giant sequoias, including the Grizzly Giant, one of the largest trees in the world.

Begin your day by driving to the Mariposa Grove and taking a shuttle to the trailhead. From there, take a hike on the Mariposa Grove Trail, which takes you through the heart of the giant sequoias. Be sure to stop and admire the Grizzly Giant, which is over 2,700 years old and stands over 200 feet tall.

After your hike, head back to the Yosemite Valley and enjoy lunch at one of the park's many restaurants or cafes. In the afternoon, explore the Yosemite Valley on foot or take a guided tour to learn more about the park's history and natural wonders. You can also rent bikes or take a horseback riding tour if you prefer.

In the evening, consider attending a ranger-led program or a stargazing event to learn more about the park's wildlife and night sky. Finish your day by watching the sunset at Tunnel View, which offers one of the best views of Yosemite Valley.

Expenses for Day 3:

- Shuttle fee to Mariposa Grove: $38 per person (includes entrance fee and shuttle)
- Lunch: $15-20 per person
- Optional activities (guided tours, bike rental, horseback riding, etc.): $50-100 per person

Overall Expenses:

Based on the itinerary above, here is a breakdown of the overall expenses for a three-day trip to Yosemite National Park:

- Entrance fee: $35 per vehicle
- Gasoline: $20-30
- Meals and snacks: $80-100 per person
- Parking and shuttle fees: $68 per person
- Optional activities: $50-100 per person

Total expenses for a three-day trip to Yosemite National Park can range from $250 to $400 per person, depending on your choice of activities and accommodations.

Accommodations:

If you plan to stay overnight in Yosemite National Park, there are several lodging options to choose from, including campgrounds, cabins, and hotels. The cost of accommodations can vary widely depending on the season and availability.

For example, the cost of a campsite in Yosemite Valley ranges from $26 to $72 per night, depending on the campground and season. Cabins and hotel rooms can cost anywhere from $150 to $500 per night, depending on the type of accommodation and season.

If you prefer to stay outside the park, there are several towns and cities nearby, including Mariposa, Oakhurst, and Groveland, that offer a range of lodging options.

7 Days Yosemite Itinerary

Day 1: Arrival and Yosemite Valley

Arrive at the park and check into your accommodations. Spend the day exploring Yosemite Valley, the heart of the park. Begin by hiking the Lower Yosemite Falls Trail, a short hike that takes you to the base of the park's tallest waterfall. After lunch, head to the Yosemite Valley Visitor

Center to learn more about the park's history and geology. In the evening, attend a ranger-led program or watch the sunset at Tunnel View.

Expenses for Day 1:

- Entrance fee: $35 per vehicle
- Gasoline: $20-30
- Meals and snacks: $80-100 per person
- Optional activities (guided tours, bike rental, horseback riding, etc.): $50-100 per person

Day 2: Glacier Point and Mariposa Grove

Start your day early and head to Glacier Point, one of the park's most iconic viewpoints. From here, you can take in panoramic views of Yosemite Valley and its surrounding peaks. Afterward, drive to Mariposa Grove, home to some of the largest and oldest trees in the world. Take the shuttle to the grove and hike the Grizzly Giant Loop Trail, which takes you past some of the most impressive trees in the grove.

Expenses for Day 2:

- Gasoline: $20-30
- Shuttle fee to Mariposa Grove: $38 per person (includes entrance fee and shuttle)
- Lunch: $15-20 per person
- Optional activities (guided tours, bike rental, horseback riding, etc.): $50-100 per person

Day 3: Tuolumne Meadows and High Sierra

Drive to Tuolumne Meadows, a high-elevation meadow known for its stunning alpine scenery and wildflowers. Hike the Lembert Dome Trail for panoramic views of the Sierra Nevada mountains. In the afternoon, drive to Tioga Pass, the park's highest mountain pass, and stop at Olmsted Point for a breathtaking view of the park's granite peaks.

Expenses for Day 3:

- Gasoline: $40-50
- Meals and snacks: $80-100 per person
- Optional activities (guided tours, bike rental, horseback riding, etc.): $50-100 per person

Day 4: Yosemite Valley and El Capitan

Spend the day exploring Yosemite Valley's western end. Hike the Yosemite Falls Trail, a strenuous but rewarding hike that takes you to the top of the park's tallest waterfall. After lunch, head to El Capitan, one of the world's most famous rock climbing destinations. Watch climbers tackle the granite face or take a guided climbing lesson yourself.

Expenses for Day 4:

- Gasoline: $20-30
- Meals and snacks: $80-100 per person
- Optional activities (guided tours, bike rental, horseback riding, etc.): $50-100 per person

Day 5: Half Dome and Mist Trail

Hike the Half Dome Trail, a challenging but unforgettable hike that takes you to the top of Half Dome, one of Yosemite's most famous landmarks. This hike requires a permit, so make sure to obtain one ahead of time. Afterward, hike the Mist Trail, a popular trail that takes you past two of Yosemite's most iconic waterfalls, Vernal and Nevada Falls.

Expenses for Day 5:

- Gasoline: $20-30
- Meals and snacks: $80-100 per person

Day 6: Hetch Hetchy Reservoir and Wapama Falls

Drive to the Hetch Hetchy Reservoir, a lesser-known area of the park but just as beautiful as Yosemite Valley. Hike the Wapama Falls Trail, a moderately difficult trail that takes you to one of the park's most stunning waterfalls. The trail offers panoramic views of the reservoir and the surrounding mountains. In the afternoon, relax and enjoy the scenery at the reservoir.

Expenses for Day 6:

- Gasoline: $40-50
- Meals and snacks: $80-100 per person
- Optional activities (guided tours, bike rental, horseback riding, etc.): $50-100 per person

Day 7: Yosemite Valley and Departure

Spend your last day in Yosemite Valley, exploring any areas you may have missed earlier in the week. Take a leisurely stroll along the Merced River or visit the Ansel

Adams Gallery to admire the park's iconic photography. Depart the park in the afternoon or evening, ending your unforgettable week in Yosemite.

Expenses for Day 7:

- Gasoline: $20-30
- Meals and snacks: $80-100 per person
- Optional activities (guided tours, bike rental, horseback riding, etc.): $50-100 per person

Overall Expenses:

- Accommodation: $1,000-1,500 (depending on type and location)
- Entrance fee: $35 per vehicle
- Gasoline: $200-250
- Meals and snacks: $560-700 per person
- Optional activities: $350-700 per person

These expenses are estimates and can vary based on individual preferences and budget. It is important to budget for park fees, accommodations, and transportation ahead of time to ensure a smooth and enjoyable trip to Yosemite National Park.

CHAPTER 4

PLANING A TRIP TO YOSEMITE

What to Pack For Your Trip

● **Clothing**

The weather in Yosemite can be unpredictable, so it is important to pack clothing that can accommodate a wide range of temperatures and weather conditions. During the summer months, temperatures can reach as high as 90 degrees Fahrenheit during the day, and drop to the 50s at night. In the winter months, temperatures can drop below freezing and snow can be common.

Make sure to pack comfortable and sturdy hiking shoes or boots, as well as lightweight clothing that is breathable and quick-drying. You may also want to pack warm layers, such as a fleece jacket, hat, and gloves for the colder months. A rain jacket or poncho is also recommended, as rainfall is common throughout the year.

● **Camping Gear**

If you plan on camping in Yosemite, there are a few essential items you will need to bring. You will need a tent, sleeping bag, sleeping pad, and a camp stove for cooking. It is important to choose a tent that is appropriate for the number of people in your group, and to make sure it is weatherproof.

In addition to your camping gear, you will also need to bring food and a way to store it safely. Yosemite has several bear-proof food storage lockers throughout the park, so be sure to plan ahead and store your food properly to avoid attracting bears.

● **Daypack**

A daypack is essential for exploring the park. It should be large enough to hold your water, snacks, extra layers of clothing, and any other essentials you may need during the day. Look for a daypack with comfortable straps and a waist belt to distribute the weight evenly.

● **Water Bottle**

It is important to stay hydrated during your visit to Yosemite, especially if you plan on hiking or engaging in other physical activities. Bring a reusable water bottle and fill it up at one of the park's many water fountains or refill stations.

- **First Aid Kit**

Accidents can happen anywhere, even in the great outdoors. Pack a basic first aid kit that includes items like bandages, antiseptic wipes, and pain relievers. If you have any specific medical needs, be sure to pack any necessary medications or medical supplies.

- **Sun Protection**

The sun can be intense in Yosemite, even on cloudy days. Be sure to pack a wide-brimmed hat, sunglasses, and sunscreen with an SPF of at least 30. Apply sunscreen frequently, especially if you plan on spending a lot of time outdoors.

- **Insect Repellent**

Mosquitoes and other biting insects can be a nuisance in Yosemite, especially during the summer months. Pack insect repellent with DEET to protect yourself from bites.

- **Camera**

Yosemite is one of the most picturesque places in the world, so be sure to bring a camera to capture all the stunning views. Whether you prefer a traditional DSLR camera or a smartphone with a good camera, make sure to bring plenty of memory cards or space to store your photos.

- **Maps and Guidebooks**

Yosemite is a large park with many trails and points of interest. Bring a detailed map and guidebook to help you navigate the park and plan your activities.

Yosemite With Children

- **Plan Ahead**

Yosemite is a large park with many different areas to explore. Before you go, research the park and decide which areas you want to visit. Consider your children's ages and interests when choosing activities and trails. The National Park Service website is a great resource for planning your trip, as well as for finding family-friendly hikes and activities.

- **Start Small**

If your children are not experienced hikers, start with shorter, easier trails. There are many options in Yosemite that are suitable for families, such as the Lower Yosemite Falls Trail, which is a flat, paved trail that leads to the base of the waterfall. You can also explore the meadows and streams around the Yosemite Valley Loop Trail, which is an easy, flat trail that is stroller-friendly.

- **Bring Snacks and Water**

Children get hungry and thirsty quickly, especially when they are active outdoors. Bring plenty of snacks and water to keep your children fueled and hydrated throughout the day. You can also stop at one of the park's many restaurants or cafes for a meal or a snack.

- **Dress Appropriately**

The weather in Yosemite can be unpredictable, so be sure to dress your children in layers that can be added or removed as needed. Bring hats and sunscreen to protect them from the sun, as well as rain jackets and umbrellas in case of rain. Sturdy, comfortable shoes are also important for hiking and exploring.

- **Use the Shuttle System**

Yosemite offers a free shuttle system that runs throughout the park, making it easy to get around without having to worry about driving or parking. The shuttle stops at many popular destinations, including the Yosemite Valley Visitor Center, Yosemite Village, and the Mariposa Grove of Giant Sequoias.

● **Learn About the Park's Wildlife**

Yosemite is home to a wide variety of wildlife, including bears, deer, coyotes, and more. Take some time to teach your children about the park's wildlife before you go, and be sure to follow all of the park's rules and guidelines for safely observing and interacting with wildlife. You can also visit the Yosemite Valley Visitor Center to learn more about the park's flora and fauna.

● **Participate in Ranger-Led Programs**

The National Park Service offers a variety of ranger-led programs and activities for children, including guided hikes, campfire programs, and Junior Ranger programs. These programs are a great way for children to learn about the park and its history while having fun and making new friends.

● **Visit the Yosemite Valley Visitor Center**

The Yosemite Valley Visitor Center is a great place to start your visit to the park. It offers exhibits, maps, and information about the park's history, geology, and wildlife. You can also purchase books, maps, and other souvenirs, and speak with park rangers for advice and recommendations.

- **Explore the Yosemite Valley Floor**

The Yosemite Valley is the heart of the park and offers endless opportunities for exploration and adventure. Take a walk or bike ride along the Yosemite Valley Loop Trail, visit the Lower Yosemite Falls, or explore the meadows and streams near the Curry Village. You can also take a guided bus tour or rent bikes to explore the valley on your own.

Night Life In Yosemite

- **Stargazing**

Yosemite is one of the best places in the world for stargazing, thanks to its dark skies and lack of light pollution. Visitors can experience the park's stunning night sky through guided stargazing programs, including the Yosemite Stargazing Tour and the Glacier Point Stargazing Tour. These tours offer a unique perspective on the park's natural wonders and are a great way to experience Yosemite after dark.

- **Night Hikes**

For those looking for a more adventurous experience, night hikes are a great option. The park offers several guided hikes, including the Full Moon Hike and the Sunset Hike, which allow visitors to experience Yosemite's natural beauty in a new light. Hiking at night also offers a chance to see nocturnal animals that are not typically visible during the day.

● **Night Photography**

Yosemite's dark skies and stunning landscapes make it a popular destination for night photographers. Visitors can capture the park's natural wonders through workshops and guided tours, such as the Yosemite Photography Workshop and the Night Photography Workshop. These tours provide opportunities to learn new skills and techniques while exploring the park after dark.

● **Nightlife at Yosemite Valley**

The Yosemite Valley is home to a range of activities that take place after dark. Visitors can enjoy live music and dancing at the Yosemite Valley Lodge, as well as night hikes and campfire programs at the Curry Village. The park also offers a range of dining options, including the Ahwahnee Dining Room, which serves up fine dining with stunning views of Yosemite Valley.

- **Night Skiing and Snowshoeing**

During the winter months, Yosemite offers opportunities for night skiing and snowshoeing. Visitors can explore the park's snowy landscape on guided tours, including the Yosemite Ski School and the Glacier Point Ski Hut. These tours provide a unique perspective on the park's natural beauty and are a great way to experience Yosemite during the winter season.

- **Nighttime Wildlife Viewing**

Visitors to Yosemite can experience the park's wildlife after dark through guided tours and programs. The park offers several night tours, including the Night Prowl and the Owls of Yosemite tour, which allow visitors to see nocturnal animals in their natural habitat. These tours provide a unique perspective on the park's wildlife and are a great way to learn about the animals that call Yosemite home.

- **Nighttime Ranger Programs**

The National Park Service offers a range of ranger-led programs and activities after dark. Visitors can attend campfire programs, stargazing events, and guided hikes, which provide opportunities to learn about the park's history, geology, and wildlife. These programs are a great way to experience Yosemite after dark and learn more about the park's natural wonders.

● **Nighttime Relaxation**

For visitors looking for a more relaxing experience, Yosemite offers several options for nighttime relaxation. Visitors can unwind in the park's natural hot springs, including the popular Merced River Hot Springs. The park also offers a range of lodging options, including cabins and lodges, which provide cozy accommodations for those looking to unwind after a long day of exploring.

People and Culture

Indigenous Communities in Yosemite

The Yosemite region has been home to indigenous communities for thousands of years. The park is situated on the traditional lands of the Ahwahneechee, who were part of the Southern Sierra Miwok tribe. The Ahwahneechee were a semi-nomadic people who hunted, fished, and gathered food in the surrounding mountains.

The Ahwahneechee people were also known for their basketry, which was made from local materials such as willow and reeds. These baskets were used for a variety of purposes, including gathering food, storing supplies, and carrying babies.

Today, the Ahwahneechee people continue to live in the Yosemite region, and their culture and traditions are celebrated through events such as the annual Indian Cultural Festival.

European Settlement and Development

In the mid-19th century, European settlers began to arrive in the Yosemite region. These settlers were drawn to the area for its natural beauty and soon began to develop the land for tourism.

One of the most significant figures in Yosemite's development was John Muir, a Scottish-American naturalist and conservationist who was instrumental in the establishment of the national park system. Muir was a passionate advocate for preserving Yosemite's natural beauty, and his efforts helped to establish the park as a protected area in 1890.

Tourism and Recreation

Today, Yosemite is a popular tourist destination, attracting millions of visitors each year. The park offers a range of recreational activities, including hiking, camping, rock climbing, and fishing. Visitors can also enjoy guided tours and ranger-led programs that provide insights into the park's natural history and cultural heritage.

Yosemite's cultural heritage is also celebrated through a range of events and festivals. One of the most popular events is the Yosemite Valley Music Festival, which features live music performances from a variety of genres. Other cultural events include art exhibitions, film screenings, and poetry readings.

Modern-Day Inhabitants

Yosemite is also home to a vibrant community of modern-day inhabitants. These include park rangers, scientists, conservationists, and artists who are dedicated to preserving the park's natural beauty and cultural heritage.

One of the most famous modern-day inhabitants of Yosemite is Ansel Adams, a photographer who is best known for his stunning black and white images of the park's landscapes. Adams was a passionate advocate for environmental conservation, and his work helped to raise awareness about the importance of protecting natural areas such as Yosemite.

Today, the park is home to a range of artists and creative professionals who draw inspiration from Yosemite's natural beauty. These include painters, sculptors, and writers who have been inspired by the park's stunning landscapes and unique cultural heritage.

CHAPTER 5

Top 10 Must-Try Best Local Cuisine in Yosemite

- **Ahwahnee Breakfast -** The Ahwahnee Hotel is one of the most iconic hotels in Yosemite, and its breakfast is a must-try. The buffet-style breakfast offers a wide selection of dishes, including eggs, bacon, sausage, pastries, and fresh fruit. The price for the Ahwahnee breakfast is around $40 per person.

- **Yosemite Burger -** The Yosemite Burger is a classic American burger, made with a juicy beef patty, cheese, lettuce, tomato, and onion. You can find this delicious burger at the Yosemite Valley Lodge or Curry Village. The price for a Yosemite Burger is around $15.

- **Half Dome Hike Lunch - If** you're planning on hiking Half Dome, be sure to pack a delicious lunch. You can order a Half Dome Hike Lunch at the Curry Village Pavilion or Yosemite Valley Lodge. The lunch includes a sandwich, chips, fruit, and a cookie. The price for a Half Dome Hike Lunch is around $15.

- **Indian Tacos** - Indian Tacos are a Native American dish made with fry bread, chili, cheese, lettuce, tomato, and onion. You can find this delicious dish at the Yosemite Village Food Court. The price for an Indian Taco is around $12.
- **Yosemite Valley Pizza** - Yosemite Valley Pizza is a favorite among visitors to Yosemite. The pizza is made with fresh ingredients and comes in a variety of flavors, including pepperoni, vegetarian, and Hawaiian. You can find this delicious pizza at the Yosemite Valley Lodge or Curry Village. The price for a pizza is around $20.
- **Yosemite Cobb Salad** - The Yosemite Cobb Salad is a hearty salad made with chicken, bacon, egg, avocado, blue cheese, and tomato. You can find this delicious salad at the Ahwahnee Hotel, Yosemite Valley Lodge, or Curry Village. The price for a Yosemite Cobb Salad is around $20.
- **Chocolate Chip Cookies** - The Chocolate Chip Cookies in Yosemite are famous for their delicious, chewy texture. You can find these delicious cookies at

the Yosemite Valley Lodge or Curry Village. The price for a chocolate chip cookie is around $2.

- **BBQ Ribs** - The BBQ Ribs in Yosemite are a classic American dish. The ribs are slow-cooked to perfection and come with a side of baked beans and coleslaw. You can find this delicious dish at the Yosemite Valley Lodge or Curry Village. The price for BBQ Ribs is around $25.

- **Yosemite Falls Salad** - The Yosemite Falls Salad is a refreshing salad made with mixed greens, strawberries, candied walnuts, blue cheese, and balsamic vinaigrette. You can find this delicious salad at the Yosemite Valley Lodge or Curry Village. The price for a Yosemite Falls Salad is around $15.

- **Apple Pie** - Apple Pie is a classic American dessert, and the Apple Pie in Yosemite is no exception. The pie is made with fresh, locally grown apples and served with a scoop of vanilla ice cream. You can find this delicious dessert at the Yosemite Valley Lodge or Curry Village. The price for a slice of apple pie is around $6.

To get these delicious local cuisines, you can visit any of the restaurants and food courts in Yosemite. Most restaurants are located within the park and are easily accessible. You can also visit the Ahwahnee Hotel or Yosemite Valley Lodge for a more upscale dining experience.

Money Matters And Saving Tips

As a tourist in Yosemite, it's important to be mindful of your money and budget. While the national park offers a variety of activities and attractions, they can quickly add up and drain your wallet. Here are some money matters and saving tips for tourists visiting Yosemite:

- **Plan ahead** - Before you even step foot in Yosemite, make sure to plan ahead. Research the activities and attractions you want to visit and determine their cost. This way, you can budget accordingly and avoid any unexpected expenses.

- **Purchase an annual pass** - If you plan on visiting Yosemite multiple times in a year, purchasing an annual pass can save you money. The annual pass costs

$80 and grants you access to all national parks and federal recreational lands for a year.

- **Use public transportation** - The Yosemite Valley Shuttle is a free bus service that operates within Yosemite Valley. It's an eco-friendly and budget-friendly way to get around and explore the park.

- **Bring your own food and drinks** - Eating out in Yosemite can quickly add up. To save money, consider packing your own food and drinks. You can bring snacks, sandwiches, and water bottles to keep yourself fueled and hydrated while exploring the park.

- **Camp instead of staying in a hotel** - If you're looking to save money on accommodations, consider camping instead of staying in a hotel. Yosemite has multiple campgrounds that offer affordable rates and a unique outdoor experience.

- **Look for free activities** - While Yosemite offers a variety of paid activities, there are also plenty of free activities to enjoy. You can go hiking, stargazing, birdwatching, or attend a ranger program.

- **Rent equipment instead of buying** - If you're planning on participating in activities like rock climbing or kayaking, consider renting equipment instead of buying it. This can save you money and prevent you from having to carry bulky equipment around.

- **Buy souvenirs strategically** - Souvenirs are a great way to remember your trip to Yosemite, but they can also be expensive. To save money, consider buying souvenirs strategically. Look for items that are unique and meaningful to you, and avoid buying items simply for the sake of buying them.
- **Use discount programs** - If you're a student, senior, or active military member, you may be eligible for discounts on park activities and attractions. Additionally, some credit cards offer rewards programs that can be used towards travel expenses.
- **Avoid peak season** - Yosemite's peak season is during the summer months, which means prices for accommodations and activities are typically higher. Consider visiting Yosemite during the off-season to save money and avoid the crowds.

Local Customs and Etiquette

- **Respect the environment** - Yosemite is a beautiful and fragile ecosystem. It's important to respect the natural environment and follow Leave No Trace principles. This means packing out all trash and avoiding disturbing wildlife and vegetation.

- **Follow park rules and regulations** - Yosemite has specific rules and regulations in place to protect visitors and the park. These rules include staying on designated trails, keeping a safe distance from wildlife, and not feeding animals.

- **Be mindful of noise** - Yosemite is a peaceful and tranquil place, and loud noises can disrupt the experience for others. Avoid playing loud music or making excessive noise, especially in campgrounds and other communal areas.

- **Respect cultural and historical sites** - Yosemite has a rich cultural and historical heritage. Be respectful of these sites and avoid damaging or disturbing them.

- **Dress appropriately** - Yosemite has a range of weather conditions, from hot and dry summers to cold and snowy winters. Make sure to dress appropriately for the weather and activities you plan on doing. Additionally, it's important to cover up in certain areas, such as the Ansel Adams Gallery, which prohibits shorts and tank tops.

- **Follow camping etiquette** - **If** you're camping in Yosemite, there are specific etiquette guidelines to follow. This includes respecting quiet hours, keeping your campsite clean and organized, and using designated fire pits.

- **Be courteous to others** - Yosemite can be a crowded place, especially during peak season. It's important to be courteous to others, whether it's allowing others to pass on a trail or being patient in lines.

- **Be mindful of cultural differences** - Yosemite attracts visitors from around the world, each with their own cultural customs and beliefs. Be respectful of these differences and avoid making assumptions or judgments based on cultural differences.

- **Respect private property** - While Yosemite is a public park, there are private properties within and around the park. Be respectful of these properties and avoid trespassing or damaging private land.

- **Practice safe driving** - Yosemite has narrow and winding roads, and wildlife can often be found on or near the roads. Practice safe driving habits, such as following posted speed limits and watching for wildlife.

By following these customs and etiquette, visitors can ensure a respectful and enjoyable experience for themselves and others. Additionally, it's important to remember that Yosemite is a shared resource and everyone has a responsibility to protect and preserve it for future generations.

Tipping in Yosemite

Tipping is a common practice in the United States, including in Yosemite National Park. As a tourist in Yosemite, it's important to understand tipping etiquette and guidelines to ensure you are showing appreciation for good service while not overspending. Here are some guidelines on tipping in Yosemite:

- **Food service -** If you dine at a restaurant in Yosemite, it is customary to leave a tip of 15-20% of the total bill. Some restaurants may include a gratuity charge for larger parties, so be sure to check your bill before leaving an additional tip. If you order takeout, it's not necessary to leave a tip, but it is appreciated if you do.

- **Housekeeping** - If you're staying in a hotel or lodge in Yosemite, it's customary to leave a tip for housekeeping. The general rule of thumb is to leave $1-$2 per night of your stay. You can leave the tip on the dresser or nightstand in your room.

- **Shuttle drivers** - The Yosemite Valley Shuttle is a free bus service that operates within Yosemite Valley. While it's not necessary to tip the shuttle driver, it is appreciated if you do. A tip of $1-$2 per person is customary.

- **Tour guides** - If you go on a guided tour in Yosemite, it's customary to tip the tour guide. The amount you tip will depend on the length of the tour and the quality of service provided. A general guideline is to tip 15-20% of the total cost of the tour.

- **Baggage handling** - If you're staying in a hotel or lodge in Yosemite, it's common for a bellhop to assist with your luggage. It's customary to tip $1-$2 per bag, depending on the weight and size.

- **Bartenders** - If you order drinks at a bar in Yosemite, it's customary to leave a tip of 15-20% of the total bill. If you order a drink at a restaurant, the tip can be included in your overall restaurant tip.
- **Spa services** - If you indulge in spa services while in Yosemite, it's customary to tip the service provider. The amount you tip will depend on the type of service and the quality of service provided. A general guideline is to tip 15-20% of the total cost of the service.

It's important to note that tipping is not mandatory in the United States, but it is customary and appreciated for good service. If you receive poor service, it's up to your discretion whether or not to leave a tip. Additionally, if you're unsure whether or not to leave a tip, it's always better to err on the side of generosity.

CHAPTER 6

TIPS AND CONSIDERATIONS

Entry Requirement

Entry fees

All visitors to Yosemite National Park are required to pay an entry fee, which helps support the maintenance and preservation of the park's natural resources and facilities. The entry fees are as follows:

- $35 per vehicle for a 7-day pass
- $30 per motorcycle for a 7-day pass
- $20 per person for a 7-day pass (for visitors 16 years and older entering on foot, bicycle, or non-commercial group)
- $70 Yosemite Annual Pass, which is valid for 12 months from the month of purchase and provides unlimited access to Yosemite National Park
- Note that these fees are subject to change, so it is always a good idea to check the current entry fees before planning your trip.

Reservations

Due to its popularity, Yosemite National Park can become very crowded, especially during peak tourist season (May through September). To ensure that visitors have a positive experience and to manage park resources effectively, the National Park Service has implemented a reservation system for certain areas of the park.

If you plan to stay overnight in Yosemite Valley or at certain campgrounds, you will need to make a reservation in advance. Reservations can be made up to six months in advance through the National Park Service website or by calling the park's reservation center. Be aware that some campgrounds and lodging options fill up quickly, especially during peak season, so it is important to make your reservations as early as possible.

COVID-19 Requirements

In response to the COVID-19 pandemic, Yosemite National Park has implemented several measures to help keep visitors and staff safe. As of March 2023, the following COVID-19 requirements are in place:

All visitors must wear face masks in all indoor public areas and on park shuttles, regardless of vaccination status. Visitors who are not fully vaccinated against COVID-19 are required to wear masks in crowded outdoor spaces and when physical distancing is not possible.

Visitors are encouraged to practice physical distancing from others who are not in their immediate party.

Some park facilities and services, such as visitor centers and shuttle buses, may have reduced capacities or modified operations to reduce the risk of COVID-19 transmission.

Visitors are encouraged to follow all public health guidelines issued by local, state, and federal authorities when traveling to and from Yosemite National Park.

Visa Requirements

If you are traveling to Yosemite National Park from outside the United States, you may need to obtain a visa to enter the country. The type of visa you need will depend on your country of origin and the purpose of your visit. For example, if you are visiting Yosemite as a tourist, you may need to apply for a B-2 visa, which is a nonimmigrant visa for temporary visitors. You can find more information about visa requirements and the application process on the website of the U.S. Department of State.

Travel Insurance

Travel insurance is an important consideration for anyone planning a trip to Yosemite National Park. Despite its stunning natural beauty and reputation as a popular tourist destination, Yosemite can be a challenging place to navigate, with unpredictable weather conditions, rugged terrain, and potential hazards such as wildlife encounters or accidents while participating in outdoor activities. Travel insurance can help protect against unforeseen expenses and provide peace of mind while exploring this iconic park.

Types of Travel Insurance

There are several types of travel insurance available to visitors to Yosemite National Park, including:

- **Trip Cancellation and Interruption Insurance:** This type of insurance covers expenses if your trip is canceled or interrupted due to unforeseen circumstances, such as illness, injury, or death of a traveler or family member, or unexpected weather events.

- **Medical Evacuation Insurance:** Medical evacuation insurance covers the cost of transporting a traveler to a medical facility if they are injured or become ill while in Yosemite National Park.

- **Emergency Medical Insurance:** Emergency medical insurance covers medical expenses incurred while traveling, such as hospitalization, doctor visits, and prescription medication.

- **Baggage Insurance:** Baggage insurance covers the cost of lost, damaged, or stolen luggage and personal belongings while traveling.

- **Accidental Death and Dismemberment Insurance:** Accidental death and dismemberment insurance provides financial compensation in the event of a serious injury or death while traveling.

Benefits of Travel Insurance

There are several benefits to purchasing travel insurance before visiting Yosemite National Park:

- **Financial Protection:** Travel insurance provides financial protection in the event of unexpected expenses, such as medical bills or emergency evacuations. This can help ease the financial burden and prevent travelers from incurring significant debt or financial hardship.

- **Peace of Mind:** Knowing that you are protected in case of an emergency or unforeseen circumstance can provide peace of mind while traveling. This can help travelers relax and enjoy their trip without worrying about potential risks or expenses.

- **Assistance Services:** Many travel insurance providers offer assistance services, such as 24-hour emergency hotlines and travel assistance. These services can provide valuable resources and support for travelers who experience unexpected challenges while in Yosemite National Park.

- **Coverage for Pre-Existing Conditions:** Some travel insurance providers offer coverage for pre-existing medical conditions, which can be especially important for travelers with ongoing health concerns.

Considerations When Purchasing Travel Insurance

When purchasing travel insurance for a trip to Yosemite National Park, there are several important considerations to keep in mind:

- **Coverage Limits:** Be sure to carefully review the coverage limits of any travel insurance policy before purchasing. Make sure the policy provides adequate coverage for potential expenses, such as medical bills, emergency evacuations, or lost luggage.

- **Exclusions:** Be aware of any exclusions or limitations in the policy, such as coverage restrictions for certain activities or pre-existing medical conditions.

- **Cost:** Travel insurance can be expensive, so be sure to shop around and compare prices from different providers to find the best value for your needs.

- **Timeliness:** Be sure to purchase travel insurance well in advance of your trip to ensure adequate coverage and to avoid potential exclusions or limitations due to pre-existing conditions or other factors.

- **Reputation of the Provider:** It is important to choose a reputable travel insurance provider with a history of providing reliable coverage and good customer service.

Read reviews and do research before selecting a provider to ensure you are making an informed decision.

Safety And Preparedness

- **Plan Ahead**

Before heading to Yosemite National Park, it is important to plan ahead and research the park's attractions, hiking trails, and potential hazards. Review maps, read guidebooks, and consult with park rangers to learn about the best routes and trails for your experience level and interests. Make sure to also check the weather forecast and be prepared for sudden changes in weather conditions.

- **Bring Appropriate Gear**

Visitors to Yosemite National Park should be prepared with appropriate gear, including sturdy hiking shoes, appropriate clothing for the weather, a hat, sunscreen, and insect repellent. Bring plenty of water, food, and snacks, and consider bringing a first aid kit, a flashlight, and a whistle in case of emergencies.

- **Follow Trail Markings and Signs**

While hiking in Yosemite National Park, it is important to stay on designated trails and follow trail markings and signs. Avoid wandering off-trail or taking shortcuts, which can lead to injuries or getting lost. Be aware of potential hazards, such as steep drop-offs or loose rocks, and take precautions to avoid accidents.

- **Be Bear Aware**

Yosemite National Park is home to black bears, and visitors should be aware of the potential for bear encounters. Store all food, garbage, and scented items in bear-proof containers, and do not leave any food or trash in your vehicle. If you encounter a bear, remain calm, speak in a calm voice, and slowly back away. Do not run or approach the bear, and do not attempt to feed it.

- **Stay Hydrated**

Dehydration is a common problem in Yosemite National Park, particularly during the summer months when temperatures can soar. Make sure to bring plenty of water and drink regularly to stay hydrated. Avoid drinking untreated water from streams or lakes, which may contain harmful bacteria.

- **Know Your Limits**

Yosemite National Park offers a range of outdoor activities, including hiking, rock climbing, and camping. However, visitors should be aware of their physical limitations and avoid pushing themselves beyond their abilities. Take breaks when needed, and turn back if you feel exhausted or unwell.

- **Respect Wildlife**

Yosemite National Park is home to a diverse range of wildlife, including deer, coyotes, bobcats, and mountain lions. Respect wildlife by keeping a safe distance and avoiding any interaction. Do not feed or approach animals, and store food and garbage in bear-proof containers to avoid attracting wildlife.

- **Carry a Map and Compass**

While many visitors rely on their smartphones for navigation, it is important to also carry a map and compass. Familiarize yourself with the map and terrain before heading out, and use the compass to orient yourself if needed. Do not rely solely on GPS or electronic devices, which may fail or lose signal in remote areas.

- **Stay Informed**

Stay informed about potential hazards and safety updates in Yosemite National Park. Check the park's website, social media accounts, and visitor centers for up-to-date information on trail closures, weather conditions, and other safety concerns.

- **Be Prepared for Emergencies**

Finally, visitors to Yosemite National Park should be prepared for emergencies. Carry a first aid kit and learn basic first aid skills, such as treating cuts, sprains, and insect bites. Carry a charged cell phone and know the location of the nearest hospital or medical facility. If you are planning on hiking or camping overnight, consider bringing a personal locator beacon or satellite phone for emergencies. It is also important to let someone know your itinerary and expected return time before heading out on a hike or camping trip.

What to Do and What Not to Do When Visiting Yosemite

DO:

- **Respect wildlife:** Yosemite is home to a variety of wildlife, including bears, mountain lions, and coyotes. Respect wildlife by keeping a safe distance and avoiding any interaction. Do not feed or approach animals, and store food and garbage in bear-proof containers to avoid attracting wildlife.

- **Stay on designated trails:** While hiking in Yosemite, stay on designated trails and follow trail markings and signs. Avoid wandering off-trail or taking shortcuts, which can lead to injuries or getting lost.

- **Be prepared with appropriate gear:** Bring appropriate gear, including sturdy hiking shoes, appropriate clothing for the weather, a hat, sunscreen, and insect repellent. Bring plenty of water, food, and snacks, and consider bringing a first aid kit, a flashlight, and a whistle in case of emergencies.

- **Know your limits:** Yosemite offers a range of outdoor activities, including hiking, rock climbing, and camping. However, visitors should be aware of their physical limitations and avoid pushing themselves beyond their abilities. Take breaks when needed, and turn back if you feel exhausted or unwell.

- **Carry a map and compass:** While many visitors rely on their smartphones for navigation, it is important to also carry a map and compass. Familiarize yourself with the map and terrain before heading out, and use the compass to orient yourself if needed.

- *Stay informed:* Stay informed about potential hazards and safety updates in Yosemite. Check the park's website, social media accounts, and visitor centers for up-to-date information on trail closures, weather conditions, and other safety concerns.

- **Be prepared for emergencies:** Carry a first aid kit and learn basic first aid skills, such as treating cuts, sprains, and insect bites. Carry a charged cell phone and know the location of the nearest hospital or medical facility. If you are planning on hiking or camping overnight, consider bringing a personal locator beacon or satellite phone for emergencies.

DON'T:

- **Feed wildlife:** Feeding wildlife in Yosemite is strictly prohibited. Feeding wildlife can lead to habituation and potentially dangerous interactions between animals and humans.

- **Leave food or trash unsecured:** Store all food, garbage, and scented items in bear-proof containers, and do not leave any food or trash in your vehicle. This helps to prevent bears and other wildlife from becoming habituated to human food sources.

- **Approach wildlife:** While it can be tempting to get close to wildlife for a photo or a better look, it is important to keep a safe distance. Approaching wildlife can be dangerous for both humans and animals.

- **Litter:** Littering is prohibited in Yosemite National Park. Visitors should pack out all trash and dispose of it in designated trash cans or recycling bins.

- **Camp in undesignated areas:** Camping in undesignated areas is not allowed in Yosemite. Visitors should only camp in designated campgrounds or backcountry areas.

- **Start fires outside of designated areas:** Starting fires outside of designated fire rings or fire pits is strictly prohibited in Yosemite. Visitors should only start fires in designated areas and follow all fire regulations.
- **Ignore weather warnings:** Yosemite is known for sudden changes in weather conditions. Visitors should pay attention to weather forecasts and heed any warnings or advisories issued by park officials. Thunderstorms can bring lightning, which can be dangerous for hikers and campers on exposed terrain. Be prepared for sudden changes in temperature and weather conditions by bringing appropriate gear and checking weather forecasts before heading out.
- **Disturb or damage natural features:** Yosemite's natural features, such as waterfalls, rock formations, and wildlife, are part of what make the park so special. Visitors should not disturb or damage these features by carving into trees, damaging rocks or vegetation, or interfering with wildlife.
- **Ignore park regulations:** Yosemite National Park has regulations in place to protect its natural resources and ensure the safety of visitors. Visitors should respect

park regulations, including speed limits, designated camping and parking areas, and trail closures.

- **Take unnecessary risks:** While Yosemite offers many opportunities for adventure and exploration, visitors should avoid taking unnecessary risks that could result in injury or death. Avoid rock climbing without proper training and equipment, and do not attempt hikes that are beyond your skill level.

By following these guidelines, visitors can enjoy all that Yosemite National Park has to offer while also respecting its natural resources and staying safe. Remember that Yosemite is a wilderness area, and visitors should be prepared for the unexpected.

CHAPTER 7

UNDERSTANDING FOREIGN TRANSACTION FEES

Avoid Cell Phone Roaming Charges

As a tourist visiting Yosemite National Park, one of the last things you want to worry about is the possibility of expensive cell phone roaming charges. However, if you're not careful, you could easily rack up hundreds or even thousands of dollars in charges for using your phone while you're there. In this article, we'll discuss some of the best ways to avoid cell phone roaming charges in Yosemite, so you can stay connected without breaking the bank.

Understand your carrier's roaming policies

Before you head to Yosemite, it's essential to understand your cell phone carrier's roaming policies. Not all carriers are created equal, and some may have more generous roaming policies than others. For example, some carriers may offer free roaming in certain areas, while others may charge exorbitant fees for even a few minutes of usage.

To avoid any surprises, it's best to call your carrier's customer service line and ask about their roaming policies in Yosemite specifically. This will help you understand what charges you may be facing, and what steps you can take to minimize them.

Use offline maps and GPS

One of the most common reasons people use their phones in Yosemite is for GPS and navigation. However, relying on your phone's GPS and maps can quickly eat up your data plan and result in high roaming charges. To avoid this, consider downloading offline maps and GPS apps before you leave home.

Google Maps, for example, offers offline maps that you can download for specific areas. Once you've downloaded the maps, you can use them to navigate without using any data or incurring roaming charges. There are also dedicated offline GPS apps, such as OsmAnd, that you can use to navigate without an internet connection.

Turn off data roaming

Another way to avoid roaming charges is to turn off data roaming on your phone. Data roaming is when your phone uses a different carrier's network to connect to the internet, which can result in higher charges. By turning off data roaming, you can ensure that your phone only uses your carrier's network, which should be covered by your regular plan.

To turn off data roaming on an iPhone, go to Settings > Cellular > Cellular Data Options > Roaming, and toggle the "Data Roaming" switch to off. On an Android phone, go to Settings > Network & Internet > Mobile network > Roaming, and toggle the "Data roaming" switch to off.

Use Wi-Fi whenever possible

One of the best ways to avoid roaming charges is to use Wi-Fi whenever possible. Many hotels, cafes, and restaurants in and around Yosemite offer free Wi-Fi, which you can use to connect to the internet without using any data. If you're staying in a hotel, be sure to ask about their

Wi-Fi policies, as some hotels may charge for access or have restrictions on usage.

When using public Wi-Fi, it's important to be cautious about your online activity. Public Wi-Fi networks can be less secure than private networks, which means that your personal information could be at risk. Avoid accessing sensitive information, such as banking or credit card details, while using public Wi-Fi.

Consider Getting a Local Sim Card

If you plan to use your phone extensively while in Yosemite, consider getting a local SIM card. A SIM card is a small chip that you insert into your phone to connect to a specific carrier's network. By getting a local SIM card, you can avoid roaming charges and take advantage of local rates.

To get a local SIM card, you'll need an unlocked phone that's compatible with the carrier's network. You can purchase a SIM card at most convenience stores and phone shops in and around Yosemite. Some carriers may require you to show a passport or other identification to purchase a SIM card.

Be mindful of your usage

Finally, the best way to avoid roaming charges is to be mindful of your usage. While it can be tempting to check your social media or email constantly while on vacation, doing so can quickly lead to high charges. Instead, consider using your phone only for necessary calls and messages, and limit your usage of data-intensive apps and services.

If you do need to use data, try to do so when you're connected to Wi-Fi or have a local SIM card. If you're not sure how much data you've used, most carriers allow you to check your data usage in their app or online account portal.

Consider an Yosemite sim card or Mifi device

Getting a Yosemite SIM card is a straightforward process. You can purchase a SIM card at most convenience stores and phone shops in and around Yosemite. Some carriers may require you to show a passport or other identification to purchase a SIM card. Once you have the SIM card, you'll need to activate it and top up your account with credit.

Benefits of using a Yosemite SIM card

- **Cost-effective:** Using a Yosemite SIM card can be much more cost-effective than paying for roaming charges. You'll be able to take advantage of local rates, which can be significantly lower than international rates.

- **Flexibility:** With a Yosemite SIM card, you'll have the flexibility to use your phone as you would at home. You won't have to worry about restrictions or limitations on your usage.

- **Convenience:** Getting a Yosemite SIM card is a straightforward process. You can purchase a SIM card at most convenience stores and phone shops in and around Yosemite.

- **Peace of mind:** By using a Yosemite SIM card, you'll have peace of mind knowing that you won't be hit with unexpected charges at the end of your vacation.

Getting a Yosemite MiFi device is a straightforward process. You can purchase a device from a local carrier or online retailer, and then activate it with a local SIM card.

Once you have the device set up, you can connect your devices to the hotspot and use them as you would at home.

Benefits of using a Yosemite MiFi device

- **Convenience:** With a MiFi device, you can connect multiple devices to the internet at once, without having to rely on your phone. This can be especially useful if you're traveling with friends or family.
- **Flexibility:** A MiFi device can be used with any Wi-Fi enabled device, including phones, tablets, and laptops. You won't have to worry about compatibility issues or restrictions on your usage.
- **Cost-effective:** Using a MiFi device can be much more cost-effective than paying for roaming charges. You'll be able to take advantage of local rates, which can be significantly lower than international rates.
- **Peace of mind:** By using a MiFi device, you'll have peace of mind knowing that you won't be hit with unexpected charges at the end of your vacation.

Choosing the right option for your needs

When deciding whether to get a Yosemite SIM card or MiFi device, it's important to consider your specific needs and usage patterns. Here are some factors to consider:

- **Number of devices:** If you only need to connect one device to the internet, a Yosemite SIM card may be sufficient. However, if you need to connect multiple devices, a MiFi device may be more practical.

- **Data usage:** If you plan to use a lot of data, a MiFi device may be a better option, as you'll be able to take advantage of local rates for a larger amount of data. If you only need to use a small amount of data, a Yosemite SIM card may be more cost-effective.

- **Type of device:** If you only need to use your phone for internet access, a Yosemite SIM card may be sufficient. However, if you need to use a tablet or laptop, a MiFi device may be more practical.

- **Coverage:** Before choosing a carrier or device, it's important to check the coverage in the area where you'll be staying. Some carriers may have better coverage in Yosemite than others.

- **Cost:** Finally, it's important to consider the cost of each option. While a Yosemite SIM card may be cheaper than a MiFi device, it may not be the best option if you need to use a lot of data or connect multiple devices.

Download Offline Map

As a tourist visiting Yosemite National Park, you may be concerned about staying connected and navigating the area. While getting a Yosemite SIM card or MiFi device can help you stay connected, it's also a good idea to download offline maps to your device. In this article, we'll discuss the benefits of using offline maps in Yosemite, and how to download them to your device.

Benefits of using offline maps in Yosemite

- **Navigation:** Yosemite National Park is a vast area with many trails, roads, and landmarks to explore. Offline maps can help you navigate the area and find your way to your destination without relying on an internet connection.

- **Planning:** Offline maps allow you to plan your route and itinerary ahead of time, without needing to access the internet while you're in the park. You can mark points of interest, hiking trails, and other landmarks on the map and plan your day accordingly.
- **Safety:** If you're planning on hiking or exploring remote areas of Yosemite, offline maps can be a valuable safety tool. They allow you to navigate your surroundings and find your way back to civilization if you get lost or disoriented.
- **Cost:** Finally, using offline maps can save you money on data charges or roaming fees. By downloading maps ahead of time, you won't need to rely on an internet connection while you're in the park.

How to download offline maps for Yosemite

- **Choose a map app:** There are several map apps that allow you to download offline maps, including Google Maps, Maps.me, and OsmAnd. Choose an app that you're comfortable with and that has the features you need.

- **Download the app:** If you haven't already, download the map app to your device from the App Store or Google Play Store.
- **Choose the area:** Once you've downloaded the app, choose the area you want to download. For Yosemite, you'll want to download the map for the park and surrounding areas.
- **Download the map:** Once you've chosen the area, select the option to download the map for offline use. The app will begin downloading the map to your device.
- **Use the map:** Once the map has finished downloading, you can use it to navigate Yosemite and plan your itinerary. The map will work even if you don't have an internet connection.

Tips for using offline maps in Yosemite
- **Download maps ahead of time:** It's a good idea to download maps to your device before you arrive in Yosemite. This way, you'll be prepared and won't need to rely on an internet connection while you're in the park.

- **Save battery life:** Using GPS and maps can drain your device's battery quickly. To save battery life, consider turning off location services when you're not using the map, or using an external battery pack to keep your device charged.

- **Mark points of interest:** Use the map app to mark points of interest, such as trailheads, viewpoints, and picnic areas. This will help you plan your day and navigate the park more easily.

- **Update maps regularly:** Maps can become outdated over time, so it's a good idea to update them regularly. Check for updates to your map app and download new maps if necessary.

Learn Basic Language

Why learn a language for Yosemite travel?

- **Communication:** Knowing basic phrases in a local language can help you communicate with locals and ask for help if needed.

- **Cultural immersion:** Learning a language can also help you immerse yourself in the local culture and connect with people in a more meaningful way.
- **Safety:** In emergency situations, being able to communicate in the local language can be crucial for getting help quickly and efficiently.

Basic language skills to learn

- **Greetings:** Learning how to say "hello," "goodbye," and "thank you" in the local language can be a good starting point for communication. In English, these phrases are widely used, but it's still polite to learn them in the local language.
- **Directions:** Knowing how to ask for directions or give directions can be helpful when navigating Yosemite. Learn basic phrases like "Where is the trailhead?" or "How do I get to the visitor center?"
- Ordering food: If you plan on eating at local restaurants or cafes, learning how to order food in the local language can be helpful. Basic phrases like "I would like a coffee, please" or "Can I have the menu?" can come in handy.

- **Emergency phrases:** It's also important to learn emergency phrases like "Help!" or "Call 911!" in the local language in case of emergency situations.

How to learn basic language skills

- **Use language learning apps:** Language learning apps like Duolingo or Babbel can be a great way to learn basic phrases and vocabulary in a fun and interactive way.

- **Take a language class:** If you have more time and resources, taking a language class can be a great way to learn the language more thoroughly and practice your skills with others.

- **Listen to podcasts:** Listening to language learning podcasts can be a good way to immerse yourself in the language and practice your listening skills.

- **Use language exchange apps:** Language exchange apps like Tandem can help you connect with native speakers of the language you're learning and practice your speaking skills.

- **Practice with locals:** When you're in Yosemite, don't be afraid to practice your language skills with locals.

They will appreciate your effort and may be more willing to help you if they see that you're making an effort to communicate with them in their language.

Cash At The Airport Is Expensive

Why cash at the airport is expensive

- **Convenience:** Airports know that they are the first point of entry for many travelers, so they charge a premium for the convenience of having currency exchange or ATM services available on site.

- **Higher fees:** ATMs at airports often charge higher fees than those at other locations, which can add up quickly.

- **Poor exchange rates:** Currency exchange services at airports often offer poor exchange rates, which means you'll get less money for your currency than you would at other locations.

- **Limited options:** At airports, you may be limited to a few currency exchange or ATM options, which can lead to more expensive fees and poor exchange rates.

Alternatives to cash at the airport

- **Use a credit card:** Many restaurants, shops, and hotels in Yosemite accept credit cards, which can be a convenient and safe way to make purchases without needing cash.

- **Use a debit card:** If you need cash, consider using a debit card at a local ATM in Yosemite. You may be able to find ATMs with lower fees and better exchange rates than those at the airport.

- **Exchange currency before you leave:** If you prefer to have cash on hand when you arrive in Yosemite, consider exchanging currency before you leave your home country. You may be able to find better exchange rates and lower fees at a bank or currency exchange service in your home country.

- **Use a travel card:** Travel cards, such as the Travelex Money Card or the Revolut Card, allow you to load money onto a prepaid card and use it like a debit card. These cards often offer competitive exchange rates and lower fees than traditional credit or debit cards.

- **Bring cash from your home country:** If you do decide to bring cash with you, consider bringing it from your home country rather than exchanging it at the airport. You may be able to get better exchange rates and avoid airport fees by exchanging currency before you leave.

Tips for saving money on currency exchange

- **Compare exchange rates:** Before exchanging currency, compare exchange rates at different locations to find the best deal.

- **Avoid exchanging small amounts:** If possible, avoid exchanging small amounts of currency, as fees and poor exchange rates can have a larger impact on smaller transactions.

- **Consider online exchange services:** Online currency exchange services like TransferWise or CurrencyFair can offer better exchange rates and lower fees than traditional exchange services.

- **Be aware of hidden fees:** When using a credit or debit card, be aware of hidden fees such as foreign transaction fees or ATM withdrawal fees. These can add up quickly and eat into your travel budget.

CONCLUSION

Tips For Solo Travelers, Families, And LGBTQ+ Travelers

<u>Tips for Solo Travelers</u>

- **Safety First:** Yosemite is a vast wilderness area with many natural hazards, including steep cliffs, swift rivers, and wild animals. As a solo traveler, you need to be extra cautious and take necessary precautions to stay safe. Always carry a map, water, food, and other essential supplies with you. You should also inform someone of your itinerary before heading out into the park.

- **Choose the Right Trails:** Yosemite has many trails for hikers of all skill levels. However, as a solo traveler, you should choose trails that are well-traveled and marked. Avoid remote or less popular trails, especially if you are not an experienced hiker.

- **Plan Ahead:** Yosemite can get busy during peak season, so it's best to plan ahead and make reservations in advance. You should also research the park and its trails beforehand to avoid any surprises or disappointments.

- **Join a Group Tour:** Joining a group tour is an excellent way to meet other travelers and make new friends. It also provides an added layer of safety and security, as you will be with a knowledgeable guide who can help you navigate the park.

- **Stay in a Hostel:** Staying in a hostel is an affordable and social option for solo travelers. Yosemite has several hostels in and around the park, where you can meet other travelers and share your experiences.

Tips for Families

- **Plan Family-Friendly Activities:** Yosemite has many family-friendly activities, such as hiking, biking, fishing, and camping. You should plan your activities based on your family's interests and ages. Yosemite also has many ranger-led programs and educational activities that are suitable for kids.
- **Stay in a Cabin or Lodge:** Staying in a cabin or lodge is a comfortable and convenient option for families.

Yosemite has several cabins and lodges that offer various amenities, such as restaurants, swimming pools, and playgrounds.

- **Bring Enough Supplies:** Yosemite has limited services and facilities, especially in remote areas. Therefore, it's crucial to bring enough supplies, such as food, water, and other essential items, to avoid any inconvenience or discomfort.

- **Be Mindful of Wildlife:** Yosemite is home to many wild animals, such as bears, deer, and mountain lions. It's essential to teach your kids about wildlife safety and proper behavior around animals. You should also store your food and other scented items properly to avoid attracting animals to your campsite.

- **Take Breaks:** Yosemite can be overwhelming, especially for kids. It's essential to take frequent breaks, rest, and hydrate to avoid exhaustion and fatigue. You should also plan some downtime and relaxing activities to help your family recharge and enjoy the park at a leisurely pace.

Tips for LGBTQ+ Travelers

- **Research the Destination:** Before visiting Yosemite, you should research the park and its policies regarding LGBTQ+ travelers. Although Yosemite is generally an accepting and inclusive destination, it's essential to be aware of any potential risks or challenges.

- **Choose the Right Accommodation:** Yosemite has various accommodation options, from campsites to luxury lodges. As an LGBTQ+ traveler, you may feel more comfortable staying in accommodation that is explicitly LGBTQ+ friendly. You can research and book LGBTQ+ friendly accommodation options online.

- **Be Aware of Local Customs:** Yosemite is located in a rural area of California, where local customs and values may differ from urban areas. It's essential to be aware of local customs and norms and respect them while visiting the park.

- **Connect with LGBTQ+ Organizations:** Yosemite has several LGBTQ+ organizations that can provide information and support to LGBTQ+ travelers. You can connect with these organizations to get tips and advice on LGBTQ+ friendly activities and accommodation options.

- **Be Prepared for Outdoor Activities:** Yosemite is an outdoor enthusiast's paradise, with numerous activities, such as hiking, camping, and rock climbing. As an LGBTQ+ traveler, you should be prepared for outdoor activities and dress appropriately for the weather and terrain. You should also carry water, food, and other essential supplies with you.

- **Be Respectful of Other Visitors:** Yosemite attracts visitors from all walks of life and backgrounds. It's essential to be respectful of other visitors' space and privacy, regardless of their sexual orientation or gender identity. You should also avoid making assumptions about other visitors' sexual orientation or gender identity.

General Tips for Yosemite Visitors

- **Respect the Park:** Yosemite is a natural wonder and a protected area. It's crucial to respect the park's rules and regulations and do your part to preserve its beauty and integrity. You should avoid littering, defacing, or damaging the park's natural features and wildlife.

- **Be Prepared for Weather:** Yosemite's weather can be unpredictable, with temperature fluctuations and sudden storms. It's essential to check the weather forecast before visiting the park and dress appropriately for the conditions. You should also carry sunscreen, hats, and other protective gear.

- **Follow Trail Etiquette:** Yosemite's trails can get busy during peak season, and it's essential to follow trail etiquette to avoid congestion and accidents. You should yield to uphill hikers, stay on the designated trails, and avoid cutting switchbacks.

- **Carry Enough Water:** Yosemite's high altitude and dry climate can lead to dehydration, especially during outdoor activities. It's crucial to carry enough water with you and drink frequently to avoid dehydration.

- **Practice Leave No Trace Principles:** Yosemite follows the Leave No Trace principles, which aim to minimize human impact on the park's natural resources. You should pack out all trash, avoid disturbing wildlife, and minimize campfire impact.

Additional Resources And Contact Information

covering over 747,000 acres of natural wonders, and as such, there are many resources and contact information available to help visitors make the most of their trip.

Visitor Centers

Yosemite National Park has four visitor centers, each offering a wealth of information about the park, including exhibits, films, and ranger-led programs. These centers are open throughout the year, with varying hours of operation depending on the season.

- **Yosemite Valley Visitor Center:** This visitor center is located in Yosemite Valley and is the primary center for visitor information. Here you can find exhibits and films about the park, and rangers are available to answer questions and provide information about trails, camping, and other activities.

- **Tuolumne Meadows Visitor Center:** This visitor center is located near the Tuolumne Meadows campground and offers information about the high country, including hiking and camping opportunities.

- **Big Oak Flat Information Station:** This information station is located near the Big Oak Flat Entrance and offers information about the park's history and natural features.
- **Wawona Visitor Center:** This visitor center is located in Wawona and offers information about the park's history and natural features, as well as exhibits and ranger-led programs.

Park Websites

The official website for Yosemite National Park is an excellent resource for planning your trip. Here you can find information about park fees, camping reservations, and park alerts. You can also find maps, hiking trail information, and tips for

vice website is another valuable resource for planning your visit to Yosemite. Here you can find information about all of the national parks, including Yosemite. The website offers information about park history, natural features, and park regulations.

Social Media

Social media platforms such as Facebook, Twitter, and Instagram can be excellent resources for learning about current events and activities in Yosemite National Park. Many businesses and organizations in the area have social media pages, and following these pages can be a great way to stay up to date on local events and promotions.

Other Resources

- **Yosemite Conservancy:** This nonprofit organization supports Yosemite National Park by funding education, preservation, and visitor programs. The website offers information about park programs, events, and volunteer opportunities.

- **Yosemite Association:** This nonprofit organization offers educational programs and volunteer opportunities in Yosemite National Park. The website offers information about park programs, events, and volunteer opportunities.

- **Yosemite Gateway Partners:** This group of local businesses and organizations supports tourism in the

Yosemite area. The website offers information about local businesses, events, and activities in the area.

- **Yosemite Hospitality:** This company manages the park's lodging, dining, and retail services. The website offers information about lodging options, dining options, and retail services in the park.

Contact Information

If you have any questions or concerns while visiting Yosemite National Park, there are several ways to get in touch with park staff:

- Emergency Services: In case of an emergency, call 911 or report to the nearest ranger station.
- Yosemite National Park Emergency Communications Center: This center is staffed 24 hours a day and can be reached by calling 209-372-0322.
- Yosemite National Park Public Affairs Office: This office can be reached at 209-372-0200 or by email at yose_public_affairs@nps.gov.
- Yosemite National Park Visitor Information: This office can be reached at 209-372-0200 or by email at yose_visitor_information@nps.gov.

Made in the USA
Las Vegas, NV
22 April 2023

70959234R00075